Y0-BCF-367

3 2711 00117 9369

ENTERED MAR 2 9 2007

Shelley Gave Jane a Guitar

Columbia College Library
600 South Michigan
Chicago, IL 60605

Shelley Gave Jane a Guitar

RICHARD MEIER

Wave Books

Seattle   New York

Published by Wave Books
www.wavepoetry.com

Copyright © 2006 by Richard Meier
All rights reserved

Wave Books titles are distributed to the trade by
Consortium Book Sales and Distribution
1045 Westgate Drive, St. Paul, Minnesota 55114

Library of Congress Cataloging-in-Publication Data:

Meier, Richard, 1966-
 Shelley gave Jane a guitar / Richard Meier.— 1st ed.
   p. cm.
 ISBN 1-933517-11-5 (alk. paper) — ISBN 1-933517-10-7 (trade pbk. :
alk. paper)
 I. Title.

PS3563.E3459S54 2006
811'.6—dc22

2006000040

Designed and composed by Jeremy Mickel
Printed in the United States of America

9 8 7 6 5 4 3 2 1

First Edition

Wave Books 006

CONTENTS

I

THE SCHEDULE

In the brush I found an oak, and sat beneath a chair.
The wife without the sign was in my mind,
the difference between being and having
has always plagued me, and the capillary action
of the air lifting darkness from the grasses.
The light doesn't change; it is defeated.
At the end of a long vagina, the constellations
tell their secrets. I'm stupid with seasons,
as the seasons are stupid with snow or flowers
or seeds in November, whatever they're given. The hair shirt
of love or power greets the day's razor
to stimulate the clouds. The test is scheduled
for every waking hour, encyclopedists. The hills echo,
every last bucket, with the last time they parted, the words and the lips,
so we could watch our going. Walking backwards is monstrous
and enormous you told me, long ago, before I knew you.

Memory of Germany

Summer of the time when things didn't happen,
the grass lay down beneath the horses. A crown of water
crowned the trees with crowns of motion,
skirts raised and shaken. There are the clouds I mentioned.

The hours filled the bag the minutes emptied.
I've done this equation. An apple hurled at the source of music
makes newer music. The lout in the cavalier house doesn't answer.
The day was made to wed the night if you were listening

by trying not to. But it was summer. It was already over.
The bus won't take you back, and there's no dancing
but above the interchanging lawn and meadow.
It's not dead, just all field flowers mowed down on top

of ones still standing. A storm came and carried away the forest.
The sun stole the space. Then I saw it.

In the Countryside

The light was on you too.
It stood there like a tongue of flame.
It made a novel. It wasn't part of your character.
It wasn't its resistance on which
the tongue foundered, a mouth in the countryside
that opened up to greet you. You admired the landscape,
later the phone call couldn't
get out of its nightgown, the novel that had escaped from its pages
when I read it, as I escaped by reading,
and loved it, white and tattered, every year from my mother.
Before you left it, leaving yourself behind like a haystack
is a hay field made human, just what I'd done to you,
you wanted to stay there forever, the ice dam that can't be predicted
giving way against the concrete pylons
floating in dismay upon the surface.

SHAKEN

I acknowledge your status as a stranger of the beautiful.
The sun is at the other end of the couch this evening
and I cannot awaken without skirting much.
He's a cad who wants to love to manage,
Lee of the beautiful, Annabel Lee of the you
thought I was sleeping because I wasn't in the room
Bishop Berkeley thought stopped existing when he left it,
which is love's generosity, like the sentence that made it
seem the milk was from the farmers
who needed cows called L 47.
When you press against their tails they think anything is possible.
So nothing can be done they grant you access.
Spread your legs to the sun is what they told us
if we were women. Otherwise blindness can take you.

Letter of Introduction

Dear Ma, my eyes are filled with sand, pillars of smoke
and the birch trees here are hollow

columns of black basalt
vomited up from the underworld.
The trash in the barn we keep until pay-day.

To debunk the book
about where things come from,
the hands of the local procuress include a boat,

birthplace of Shelley and Hermes,
chaos shimmering through

the veil of order,
the drainage ditch outlined in tulips

where I saw them not, and was not heard.

Various Configurations

It's the beginning of a novel, the deckled edges green and silver,
the oily brown center of a drab March cornfield seen close up
but in motion, from the seat of a bicycle. Next the child
begins to shake his head in a ballad
by Dexter Gordon, *a strange music to offer*
as the mother cross-writes in a letter, conserving
herself in herself, as she gave it to him, years earlier.

But that wasn't what had happened. Maybe it had,
but it wasn't *here*.
The cornfield remained drab because of March,
but that wasn't its essence,
and the child shook, and the music played,
separate as her pleasure in the color from the tractors
and man with a gun, the small pout of shot
with its sharp echo, and then a pair of crows drawn
up in curves as if on strings out of the wood.
It didn't amount to the whole when the parts
weren't deficient. The music stopped in the expectation.

It was like a sound that rose up out of objects
when you looked at them. The tin can of the silos
or the booming of the open railroad cars
as they sat in suspension at the base of the hill,
seeming to absorb the suddenly brilliant southwestern clouds
into a previous hour. One thing was always dragging
a foreign perception out of another, he with she,
or she with child. It was hard to be so transfigured.

And yet, for all the lines, there was the air and a body.
Even if you couldn't say which was which.
The little mountain of the snowbank was blotched
with veins of dry grass and leaves. They seemed to cover
and muddle the still white snow. It was gradually failing
until the grass and leaves were to be what was
revealed, before any other renewal. He would be grown before
they understood him, or knew each other, and the thing
they'd wished away, to better see, would remain
in all its purity. It meant to be loved forever.

What Tomorrow Looks Like

The bouquet isn't open
in the tulips, but the blossoms
from the service bush stagger
the eggs in the basket

on the arm of he who ventures
along the path of Ands laid out in the loam
of the asparagus cooks quickly,
where the monk quietly, why the distance negotiably

between being and having. The antlers
of the ghosts of young peach trees prostrate
yourself with orchard
to be pleasure, disorder. I crossed out all the other letters,

the sound between the thunder and the lightning,
and the names of things on the page, like pilgrims.

POST HOC

If you stand on the bathtub, the tree in the courtyard.

If the vernal equinox,
if long since over and approaching again
to launch into another summer, like a swollen gazebo
with no people haunts the park on the corner.

The plates rattle. The pink chair
in the morning sun from the take-it-or-leave-it
house better known as the dump, the vernal equinox
in our unshared vocabulary, yours and mine depending.

If you think about experience, I didn't do anything,
or deep-seeded unhappiness,
the vernal equinox is on the calendar with the turning of the pages,
long since over and long approaching
again is in the form of a dream that it was all a dream
about leaving the cave, known by the dump, effluvia,
effluvium, to launch into what's already another
summer the quartz warhead of the great farm
of the unfenced prairie, illegible shredded grasses,
a habit for butterflies, where no people haunt the corner
of the fat gazebo a cloud at the slight rise
sent out to meet you, sorry to have fallen out of

touch, the plates rattle, the tree in the courtyard,
the scrim of voices that shadow our every action
long since over and approaching the end,
the take-it-or-leave-it pink chair
better known as the sun that bisected the trunk,
a splay-fingered birch on the first edge of summer,
better known as the dump, about to be launched
into without moving as the vernal equinox approaches,
the glide along the sidewalk toward a fat gazebo,
below a full moon, the unfortunate design,
the pleasure of the trance, habitat where no people
from where you are haunt the corner
where you are, if you stand on the scrim of voices,
voices not of those present, at the moment they are present,

if you think about experience,
long since over launched into another summer,

in the pink chair sitting
in the sun in the tree in the summer, bisected,

in the courtyard.

Proposal

Wildflower honey, bouquet, fish water, melon
in the hoop house, seed and seedling doubt
teach, and three days the puckerbrush
the minor plum into oblivion casts. It would be sweet
to die until tomorrow, plum, crumble
soil block with weed, footnote out the senses.

Faith doesn't know how to spell the conditional.
That gerund holds you captive, a fish smell
fertilizing all those people you hate, the black yew
stalking the meadow, where the cat holds still for hours,
hunting the disease that brought him to the nest.

The need to get it out seemed like the past
and the future, the pepper in her palm
and the tongue presaging weeds, in 25-cent vases,
but it is the decision to be part of our lives,
people around the kitchen table, don't you think?

CLIMACTERIC

You make your house a boat or die,
the water of your lifetime rising,
a child you don't remember having,
and have to escape, take with you. Virtue

is left in the grass, what once was the grass, as what one does,—
I put a slip of paper in the water for a boat—
with the sound of a bird's nest in August,
shell empty to the tree,—

and watched it float toward shore then sink
and then slide out in a deeper current,—
the children are hungry and can't be fed
or even described. The light in the strings of a shopping cart play
the huge floating as it waits and waits.

It was from that sweet/sad fathom I read the line I knew
mingled with love and then dissolved in sound,
no question from that vacant window but a crack,
through to the river to which the banks do violence

and the sea full of shells. The wind can't come,
it's below us now, which the night that followed sung
from your persistence. The disastrous spread
of continents and language. It was what I would have known

had I let the thought take hold, I imagined,
of the need not to move, a terror of the first order
thrown over into blur, if this should reach you,
although no thought inform,
old and beautiful, dying to be still.

MY SECRET LIFE

The rain that cuts makes motion less
and more exact as you find yourself a little further
along than expected, the river on both sides of the pier,
but moving one direction. I was made to get down on my knees, I can't believe
I ate her present, what's your favorite book of the bible,
we heard without wanting an answer,
made by the world into something beautiful, the name
that rings in the ear in sleep and is your own and someone else's,
though no one said it—because of that—at least not consciously.
That lack of consciousness has always seemed to signal
something true, like a plate with a flower painted on it
emerges from the dirt floor of an abandoned house.
You said what you'd been longing to:
I never would have come here without you,
and now that I have, no other course of life is possible,
at least in the present, which comes into my mouth
just as these impressions leave it, or the light goes out of faces
as they steel themselves to meet the camera. It was filming
all along, before they knew it.

Then what happens? Snow accentuates
the spikes of weeds. It softens the tiny, extreme
danger, and the lack of wind, ourselves
inching into the world to be admired.
The frost on the leaky uninhabited farmhouse window,
with busted pipes and rotting antiques, really does
curl like the fossil of a fern from the surrounding wetland,
so we can continue being ignored as outmoded
as we are told is the sublime, listening then
without being subject, as behind the psychiatrist I read
on the divided ceramic head *love* and *approbation*,
though it wasn't legible from that distance. The patterned back of an overcoat
in the pink filigreed half-light, by the park where you'd been walking
early for the encounter, is internal, a ring slipped onto a finger,
the snow raising footprints, a real out-of-body experience
that began inside the head, placing the ecstasy in how it got out, shaken
as the bird that doesn't, for once, hit the window

but flies straight into the house, confused and shaken,
wrapped in a sheet through which a hand feels
its heart beating, and lets it go, the person surprised and laughing
a little to have remained, your mouth full and beautiful,
unsure to whom it must address this question
about being a threshold, as if to speak will contradict
or prove it when neither, in the breeze and moon-like streetlight
filtering through the curtain, is possible. It's true
as you want to be, and are, though a step away from then,
already what it was, watching the snow fall
with an exaggerated effort, its ribbons laced into the trees,
keeping you confounded.

LAKE BATHING

The water green with orange fire as a box
of turquoise from the mine
cut us into patches for a quilt
we made to lie down in as a part. Alone,

solitary were three words that came to mind
with people otherwise called
learning to swim, binding the water to our limbs
until they overflowed with flowing grains and fell

to my brother, and my sister to me.
Reek and commencement strayed from the surface,
something due to the past to return we borrowed:
despite these words, I too am a person.

THE BIOGRAPHY OF GRASS

And now that I love you it has to be
true or something more moving
but the problem then was that everyone loved me
for expressing these ideas we could all agree on
like a cloud posing for a shepherd or a column
in the middle distance before the sky of the painting.
The was a way to get them to shut up so
I could write a name in the sand of the voluptuous
and keep up our spirits for the long night
which had long been promised to be beginning.
And now that I love you like a column
or a shepherd posing as a cloud tending
the middle distance so close you can reach out and touch it
because you are prevented and go along with,
the you that's I, the changeable which isn't inter,
which the fire refutes, it's on fire, and the lines on the clock,
it's elaborate, consent to number the matted grasses
into the outline of the two of all the billions
that happened to collapse, and didn't need preserving.

November

Covered in straw, the last of the sun
or the stars at first,
before you can see them.
We have to include both of them.

We have to acknowledge the thought about the thing
that happened before it did,
the thought before the thing, and then the thing,
and then again the thought,

that we could know it. We were chosen
to lay my head alone on the pink chair leaking
a white like snow and stained with rings
of mud absorbed like geese into the river

silver rings, and see this and report it as
the blue of the black leaves left on the oak
after dusk
made black by blue behind them having white,

sun down and stars not yet making points,
to see this and report it, to you completing
the transaction with the spirit
by letting it continue.

To the Living

It's getting kind of dark to wash the car.
This was during the railroad track on night,
the full moon during the civil wars,
up all night with a halo for an obstacle.
Coming of age the baby spoke
in the dream I heard the war
and woke up in a bush, an earth berm or ship to the exact
tune of that summer on the slate in the great city
known to have been spared a thousand years
of roots spread through the bridges.

The need I had to fill out a form everyone shared
she woke on the night when Venus
was a plane from the east.

During the telephone pole with its four zoas
under the civil war
the frog and the dung beetle
went unremembered.
We are become a victim to the living
shooting west for exploration.

I'd never seen the insects in the arc light.
I took up that image
out of frustration, the civil war, the railroad
tracking moonlight, economic effects of depression on the economy,
the four sides of the floodlit stone house on the hilltop
walking by slowly while the moon was become
a face in the division of the branches,
the beasts of the day broke in in tongues
in small black bugs in the tight buds imagining
the fruit in the long green sink of April, cracked and under
water, folded in the body for a period, a narrow house
can't be turned over, opened there, and put away
and later to be identified, between the ties and indefinite gravel,
on the rail that leads out during the river, the berm
become a trestle from the war, a few flowers dangling, taped
to its outside edges, a note without which we'd be stuck here,
shoes and seep water, staring at that outside world.

2

February

The sun is in the room again now where you left it
above the chair with your head in it that autumn
before you'd returned the letters to the dead which
had come from them and begun the plural
fucking with the one-to-one dearest
ratio among all the voices (I refused to record in my diary
what we were saying). It was like a head shaking,
the sun through the great no of the seasons, or looking over each
shoulder into two lights on the west-sloped fields east of the sick
and, the sleeping *how*, each ear of the baby year divided
in the middle called two different people.

The children were running back toward the Parkview
School they just got out of, dragging luggage
in the space between the ground before the thinking.
It should have returned by all rights to the ordinary.
Instead looking through one tree the other is illuminated
crossed with what we can know of on another. I didn't touch you,
as the mind comes to prefer. I felt my hand taken from me.
Like a waist held across a yard, the grip closest to the eye,
the sentences were so clear you had to run into them
and discover your head in the sliding glass door
of the house on stilts, sleeping on water in the center of the marsh
short lyric stories of love frozen in the still
it wasn't a body of water between the trees' front lawn
caught in a finger-hole, meant to animate the book.

FOR OBSCURE BUT CONVINCING REASONS

The essence of a thing goes on and off like a switch.
Eventually I don't believe in figuring things out,
and I just know there is a problem without that benefit,
however dubious it must always be. It's part of
the way I sit down on the couch, part of the pattern
to make his fingernails scratch against the fabric, a damask
50/50 furniture garment on sale last summer.
That, too, is a kind of seeing. This one particular minister
or official was blind and nearly run out of the government
for, some said, not seeing another woman. I put that
on the form in the place set aside for a brief biography,
including education, awards, experience, and
as if the motion in the string of lights was genuine and not
an impossible to resist flashing order.
I was halfway to the post office to burn my draft card
long after I knew I wouldn't do it when I saw
what I see, the boy everyday coming home from high school.
The conjunction prevented anything different,
and I was heading home before I knew it
when the ground began to sing beneath the mountains
of corn beside the corn factory. It was my independence
I questioned, was it still desirable in the face of these marvels, the eye in the knotted
plywood table, and the dancing to unheard music? No.

The Shame of Fools

Two geese veered off the river above the ballfield.
If it flowed in the right direction, I'd already met you,
and yet it's still possible life continues, inside the reference to death,
is less of a hassle here, as she so bluntly put it, removing dust and Asian beetles
from the Venetian blinds with a flick of her fingers.
The rooms are completely updated, a walk-in closet
that used to be a bedroom. You can imagine people sleeping there,
and reasons why it's empty.

Others had disappeared by morning in the congenital acrimony
of waking in the arms one had gone to sleep with, the lace of the nightgown
folded with light through the curtains into a Russian fairy tale
rushing to repeat its past and bring us, yet again,
into the present of the story. And it's enough to imagine you can also,
living here finally, in a small way looking through the willow at the schoolyard,
the afternoon sun caught, as it was then, in the equipment,
and then from the enclosed summer porch toward the enormous girth
of the grain depot one might feel small, and well-placed,
far from the crushing touch of others, sure to be a star
in the latter chapters, free, in that sense, and of your origins.

A tradition started and we lived in a house
that expanded like a uterus in space instead of people.
The tradition was invented on a day like this one
when the hilarious thing about the dream was the dreamer
not knowing why the pirates had attacked him
in broad daylight the width of a river bluer
than the tradition become a tradition
in the dimming of the day of its conception,
a day bright like a fish with conception,
and so passed on like a child to the child dreaming,
not the child anymore, her grandmother every night
reveals to her the masque of sitting up in the curtain
of a room we had blindfolded, to control the space of that house with people,
to make her live in the compound, maybe dead or heaven.
But it was the child who dreamed the house smaller
by expanding to accommodate people, the tradition entrenched
in the loss of origin, the dream's hilarity unable
to climb out of knowing why it happened.

Villanelle

The psalm behind
my eye kept twitching. I dreamed you came to see me.
I dreamed there was a man who must have been you.

Conversation wears a bustle—I never wanted to step foot on
the continent—and the switching of the body—switch switch—
was the snare drum of a grace step.

I'm a puss willow among dead
stumps whose roots have drownded. Or could it have been a fire? Your eyes are the color
of evergreen bark in winter light drifts. Your eyes are the color

of lower down the trunk in shadow. Layers that show the century
as undergarments fashion us out of snow shifts.
I was cold a long time before we traded personages,
and knew there was no one in the bed to receive them.

It was an actual weight pressing down on me.
It was really we who had finished our duties elsewhere.
The real villanelle was the situation
in the moment it had forsaken.

Consulting the Oracle

I.

A bird from the bracken, a thing from the explosion.
Did we ever talk about lemons? Sex-warmed breezes
found a rose could hold a parking lot—know that one?—
to heaven like the 97 strands of wire in each cable,
of which a man's made up of thousands, like a concert.
But it's impossible to return it now
that it's been lived in. It's the über-division of the spoils
into stains. You think you'd like to taste one?

II.

The sea was in the sheets, between all the lips
the sex was given to you thus, a broadside
hidden in a wilting paper boat by being sunk,
balloon with cow gum, spirit lamp flown,
on the side of a barn, hammer, nail, given a passing
on the road, a bottle in waves to read
the declaration of the rights of *I don't know,*
salt trial of the monarch versus who
had been preparing for the house to grow a loom,
woven out of a doom into distress and given
and then out through the mistress heard a form
of hanging beads the flies were baffled and then the given
fig cicada culvert swell lemon torn
tomb bell on the garden wall tongue learns.

III.

The children play on the river of swans they don't know when
they'll die out of curiosity, siblings they haven't met
yet long enough to understand. There's beer in the tulips, Sun,
in the Baptist churchyard, a ram's head on a beautiful
body doesn't know when. The first time I stood up the tulips closed
the afternoon in north-by-northwest wind, a glacial moraine
behind the diner, huge inspection. The future consecrates,
whatever it looks at, the field glasses in which the swans consist of
getting bigger, during the yearly break-up of the river,
either from a boating accident or swimming too quickly.
What is this beautiful you keep, while it tries the unremembered?

IV.
Is the dream child really easier to handle?
Blood runs in a cavern.
I can't believe we have to teach under the table.
Four is a minor number and harder to sing
so change the lyric to the grass yields to the body and rises
through the snow, because the beloved's the one you can
imagine. Is that so awful? Down at the dump
they've got a house for books. Do you know if that's actually part of it?

THE FIG TREE

In the dream of three
the hummingbird behind my back was me
and your eye like a large apple
drinking into it. Settled above the river
the great blue heron excretes, you're actually going to use it,
a white dream of numbers equaling
something sensual, the screen roof of the lanai
a ball of rain sliced into mist
stared at and called into answer
in a dream of these pink panties
falling from the sky accident
after their origin in the sun-driven.
The ocean (the sea) stacked between
three white railings wore your hat
except where the straw was woven diamond black
and you and she were integers.
The fig trees do have leaves like genitals!
The green fruit is the black fruit, across imaginary borders.

"When a child begins to read history one marvels, sorrowfully,
to hear him spell out in his new voice the ancient words."
—Virginia Woolf, *Jacob's Room*

I.
The little light of the mind supported the comma
he found among the leaves. The spaces turned
green and yellow to describe how he saw it,
and then a whole woman among the branches.
I am not here, they said, the second before he chose
to blur the leaves for her. The light bulb

knocked out by the word D. H. Lawrence preferred
for fucking. The light helps the darkness,
a reason for the curtains. So the darkness helps the light,
he answers,

the abyss of non-being—the name made him
think of Shelley and the sea on which one floated,
a girl in a tree. He felt the problem.
The dark of the moon on the new floating down,
being the sea on which they floated, the comma between them
when they came, it was only one thing really.
He would like a picture of when he sees her.

II.
The manure shone in the cart behind the tractor,
the water in the stream that appeared in winter,
on a bed of orange slush and soil. My thumb,
the baby says, pointing at the man's.
That was just a dream he had, though he knows it's true,
by which he means approaching
light in the snow-struck furrows, the words for the colors
when he saw and thought of colors, and so on.

I felt your teeth, she said. There isn't a word there.
She sat, the dry edge of the road, to feel the sun half on her.
Like when I close my eyes to face him.
And if it happens to be true, she said. The seven white children
became two Holsteins. It was a sign for the dairy.
Did she want a picture of how he'd felt to her?
A chicken in the broken pane of the chicken house

showed them how they felt. She used to buy eggs here.
She'd undone the knot for him when his hand came
and she'd undone it. It was yesterday, tomorrow.
She laughed. But it's a good smell, isn't it?

Fox in Summer, Stole in Winter

I love the grasses in the winter. That's why we plant them.
To look through the cattails, the sun flares,
and the way they cling to themselves like animals.

The grasses in winter get whiter and whiter.
I take back what I said about being sorry.
If it's air or fire or water, it'll be fine,

or we'll have to struggle. I've never walked in the stubble-fields
or gleaned the soybeans, but just to look at them.
It isn't possible to be farther away from life out here,

only closer. The white skirt was yellow, for example,
and I couldn't have planned the green grass of summer.
Add it to the list of things I'll never say again,

the foxtail in a jar, for want of how I said them then.

Bibliomancy #238

Broke, the blue glass broke the statue of the snow in education,
broke the sick rose into starlight untenable for reading
the alphabet of planting. The clods broke into hands,
there was a really good amount of worms. You plotted

against the pattern, I held the root-heads in the soil.
Limestone in the lower orchard broke the dream against a pick-axe
struck a wall below the surface. You lay me in a furrow, lay
yourself the rose light in the turning, dark field

of the tenable, unburied, unbereft, unbroken, the nightcrawler
in two pieces describing the blade of spade or shovel.
Water sloshed in the truck bed, stones were animate in removal,
and it was better to stand than fall from the hay bales, neck broken

with the duly elected, when the driver stopped short, laughing,
stiff with envy for his strange, sweet action.

Endless Topic

There's no one in this poem.
That's the wine talking. That's the
phlox in the field undressing
the fescue with purple clusters. I love what's beneath you.
And the office carpet

has a carpet I love to cover it.
It feels better without not hurting,
like a fart brings your beauty to life
galloping around the field with branch antlers.
She loved him enough to make him marry

Mary, he her enough not to do it.
Between her legs he tasted iron.
There's no one in this poem to touch your penis
or listen to your clitoris. The water rises
around the debt of the body. There's no body

left to serve the sentence, the icon of the state
long since become a face,
in an antique skirt, no underwear
on the driest hundred acres. A bandanna
on my face and the sun on your

equality, to live in the field where a stick has fallen,
I just wanted to hear your voice,
not letting it be touched, or in this
that came toward you but never crossed that mystic border.
Then something did happen.

3

YOUR DREAM REDACTION

Someone had long ago painted the plaster
behind the white and green floral paper a climbing flower,
a morning glory. The dark green stem in black edges,
the same as the dark pink blossoms,
twists them into opening, the edge of the letters
or a body in prophecy,
the passage in a book that existed once,
and is now the wish to find it.

Thus a sky of blue enameled tiles
in the construction dump on the way to town
and the bird of a bit of palm
the sea tossed up and out. The puppets talked
in the three aspects: angle of the faces, your hands, like an old woman's
slid up inside the flowered dresses, male and female
snipped directly from the bolts of cloth.
And the most terrible rainstorm there began with dust,
where you bit a peach, in the shade of the Temple of Hera
where Shelley gave Jane—a guitar!

thinking, I need to see the calves,
the river continued, flowing south over the apparent
floating of the river bottom, clear water encasing,
enabling like a glacier receding in spasms up a mountain,
the ones who missed and waited
in the shadow of the plane trees outside the ancient
fortifications on either side the wheat field.
He's inside you, she answered, redaction
of the sky into a child, the sea, peach, tile
ascending like the sea wall into puppets
on all our hands the child watched and waited
as the musician can accommodate his voice to the sound of
the guitar I gave you from a great distance
by seeing the bodiless mind of the peach pit floating
in eclipse of the winding sheets of light
in which the sea appeared as the edge gone dark
from the forge, a thing (no song!) which can be touched.

A sparrow over the street lamp like a ball tossed,
the red-winged blackbird took its place in the maple
to the man pedaling in a gentle weave his course
from the eggs laid in the nest of weeds in the shoreline clatter
of reeds and cattails. The spider plant was in blossom
with six unlikely white mannerist petals below six gold-tipped pistils,
and a single white one had splayed its bearings.
But the feeling evades you, a leaf turns cartwheels on the screen,
daughter of Charon the boat-seller, and your own beloved self!

Lawrentian ABCs

About noon on Monday the daffodils opened
because you happened to be watching, thinking they were tulips
concealed in the green leaves until they trumpeted
dumbly like Apollonaire's bridges.
Evening employs the gentle roar of a steam engine passing.
Forgive me. It's the pipes, like
golden light transmutes
his and her body parts into flame and
I can't say anything but us has been transported.
Jealous of ourselves we realize this,
killing the tulip (one has opened) almost in our embrace,
like I swallowed the Ls in swallow, but you could see it.
Mondrian didn't hate trees for loving boogie-woogie,
nor is the crack in the tulip not the way we see it, or the tongue enters.
OK,
present company exalted. The
quickening
ratio of night to day on the
sundial of the tulip sleeping from your lips
twins
us.
Vacantly the moon
waxes as space wanes into
X, the algebraic dress the wind lifts.
You look like a tulip, my chosen
Zed.

Answering You

Abracadabra. You return from exile and enter
blue, barely concealed beneath night and a bathrobe. The shape of
comfort is the title of a book never published, consequently
defying non-
existence. The definite lines of a tree in
fog forget hiding in exchange for a flood of space
God calls you. My
harangue continues like, was it Mary Pickford? on the
ice floe heading toward the waterfall. The birth of a nation
jumps floe to floe to save her dark eyes just in time for her
kindled gaze to strike the camera.
Longing for you I thought of her, proving
multiplicious all singularity. Well,
Nuncle, the morning is dark as night behind these eyeshades.
O won't you lift them and grant me the
placebo of waking on a flood plain to flood warnings.
Quiet. The last copies of
radical love lie burning in the novel.
Somebody said it didn't exist. It was you
telling me you were still sleeping, like a crocus
undoes winter's blouse until it shivers, both of them
violently.
Why
Xenephon chose the high ground? To come down to
zero.

CERTAINTY

Why does the ice shifting like a cloud in the current,
the sky brought down to the planet, make the pleasure
of standing uncertain, and standing uncertain on the solid
pier of treated wood a pleasure, a certainty in the continental

drift of the thinnest sheet of ice, a sheet that breaks
when pulled over the face or the body, the body of the river,
the sky's face in it, the dog's foot on it breaking through,
the geese and ducks walking as if out of the book

onto the table beside you? The bones, the popcorn
and crackers, the inducements to meaning, to stopping,
you sounded clear until I said it was so. Observing
or being observed, the masks slipped for a moment,

the cow hesitated on the threshold of the latest pasture,
the mountain rested in the hill, the sky got darker
than the shifting river. Winter was far behind
in winter, said in the depths of the argot.

MY FAVORITE THOUGHT

The spray hungers to be a rose.
It is one. The silk trembles to be an arm,
the arm locks itself unto a rose . . .
there are two ways to be discovered. At tea time
we were interrupted by a washstand
before the crucial word could be spoken.
In the trees the empty spaces made a door
and saw us out of them. What is it
you'd like a cup of? People escape from their
clothes, and you escape into them,
as the fly in the baseboards in winter sings
more slowly the tree in summer,
and the long, white neck turns green with water.
This was called dying, or being alive, swimming on top of
what swims or lives or dies inside you, I'm so glad to have met you
off the prow, and the man overboard approaching.

WHAT

The maple in leafless winter, red-tipped branches,
I couldn't tell if it was a man or a woman,
but it was you I wanted the body thought.
The water in leafless winter,
the water frozen in the birdbath,
if the thought of the man or woman,
thought the body of the red-tipped branches.
The first day of spring is leafless winter.
The nest hangs by a hair, but I couldn't
do anything about it, in the wind and
hard and wet in leafless winter.
The body thought the body was taking precedence.
They're buying it to do a tear-down.
I'm walking on my head, relieving the body.
The voices sound like engines.
Wet and hard is thought of the body.
Betrayal of the pasture in leafless winter,
I sat on the couch
and red-tipped the branches. I busied the water.
I listened, the tear-down. The water in the bird-bath,
the truth in leafless winter, red-tipped, untold,
a man or a woman, the thought of the body,
the branches, the water, like an engine.
It was the body thought the body wanted
the red-tipped branches.

HÖLDERLIN TURN

The lantern born in the dark, the boat
with the load of wood, you can't see,
what you must think beside the small tower—
It gave shelter to a man once,
and you found a place near the church to overlook,
the city, the path by the river where you saw—
It gave shelter to a man once,
to a woman and a book supported by the gate
which had to oppose it, through which we entered,
the flame rolling in the shaken boat, the people
looking up at the tower in the dark,

It's promiscuity that does that, raises the risk of being unhappy
where one is, like a pennant, a skirt in the sun by the farmhouse,
not owning the space. Your breast and your mouth
said tulips. The tulips said, forget this. You came in a truck,
in the grass outside the window on the bed. Before the lease expired,
it was month-to-month, and we knew it was a matter of not giving notice.
How easy burns the winter on the first clear day.

I couldn't help but see it when I closed my pen and the letter
I'd been writing, dark blue where the current tore the ice.
The tax collector proceeds independent of that, and the civil union
of red and white on the winter porch. Minds
touched, and they might have been ours,
but either way. We looked back on them as if they were,
and when they flew away, winter didn't continue,
it came back to life as we recognized the difference.

If you can grasp that the flight of a lantern in somebody's hand,
I was strumming the guitar
and there were times when my hand was lifting away from the strings,
a student, probably, is no hard thing, even
if to call it music is unwieldy, is not untrue.
A duck flies straight up through a juniper
or the need for adult supervision. We were probably recorded leaving
without the kids, to spend our days in a tower
at what used to be the edge of the city. Things become central.

The youngest are in the kitchen making jam,
monitoring the temperature in copper kettles, adding sugar.
The time the kitchen burned down we were right there watching,
we the younger, a column of black smoke and fire,
and for the next few weeks we lived around it
as one does with a ghost or a videotape found in the rafters
in the years before VCRs. But eventually we're going to have to watch it,
the boat continued, the bed-wetting and long dinners
punctuated by cries of equilibrium. The sun climbs,
the British begin to learn to foxtrot, and it's the awkwardness
I recognized, as something I'd known forever and
would return to frequently. In a pinch a clump of leaves
can serve, a hole in the side of a barn, a famous date
in history or the year of your birth.

Dream Essay

Thus Plato's Republic is thrown out of the poet,
where, point by point, like a crown, or a star,
it may continue. This is the idea of happiness,
understanding what God meant by the word
pain, as the painful quiz (it *is* what's graded)
is followed to a discussion in which one is free
to drift finally like a lily anchored to the muddy bottom,
or chickens emerging from the shadows at your arrival;
the hawk who sits on the unseen branch
feasting on your sister couldn't stand your presence.
And as to put it this way just cheapens the experience,
it's the past that changes, the river that's been here for years,
and has already stoically outlived us
no matter how often replenished.

But one feels good to be bored by pornography,
moved by the living, and make of it all an idea
that's less important, dissolving the equation
where I was accomplished. Three parts are unified by death,
the boy who is a boy or a vision,
the lovable murderer, the doomed lovers, but people
don't talk through the opera, or shouldn't,
meaning they do, they do but softly, like people
in bed without pride, or worse or better,
then frightened waking, and then the place it touches
being gone, the windows closed by rain, what was the wind in the aspens.

The Myth of Renewal

It is going to change, only not into what it was
or had been imagined to be, and wanted,
and then thought couldn't come again,
the one asleep and the one awake in the infant light,
blinking at the dream that seemed to have ended
at the top of the stairs, bright gray in the corner where she lay
as if in sleep, though he was just as startled.

I thought after I'm dead this will continue, though with the rows
ploughed under and replaced, beaten down by rain and lifted by wind
and beaten down by sun,
mingled together in order to be sifted apart.

Nights I closed my eyes onto that kaleidoscope,
and failed to turn away these dreams imprinted from without.
I'm too large, the house thought, the curtain drawn
to reveal the shifting pattern, the perpetual child,
its temporary name and fixation on change and certainty,
and another to witness it, and a third to acknowledge
something had descended, a fourth
that the desire for death was the instinct
to care for what had been laid at one's feet, however it seemed,
and an inkling in the failure to change
to change anything.

HER THEORY OF CATHARSIS

A white circle spray-painted in the grass
and filled for rabbits with poisoned corn
or an operation of chance or some other means
to which I was not privy. I followed the white arrows
of the cross-country course between the woods and crops
where the tractor moved imagining I too
was being compelled to finish before the companies
began to collect seed patents after world war two
and more and more the strains of families vanished.
The two looking back saw only trees while to those above
the contact between them and the intimate mood
were hardly avoidable. Why had we come to the hotel
was what I thought as I held my arms out
as though I were one of the characters in the book who kept
asking that. These rural streets had seemed like Paris
listening to a song and looking up into blue clouds in the evening.
I was anywhere, having solved the problem of moving,
and the characters would simply speak their lines hanging laundry
or in the grocery store, unifying place by action,
so that later in a dark room I could assemble them.

Evening, Various People

I.
Raised behind the pages of a book
and a hand-drawn map it reproduced
I got more lost in the more I knew

the doors of the houses and the woods laid flat
in the fields to be seen were looked up through,

you won't mind if I talk about my personal life now,
a pack of lies started circa night
when you forced a path between waistband and skin—

space appeared where there had been none,
a hand to occupy it and then the space
became material whether something had been

taken or removed was like a man
"of white turned upside down
became his hat and berry-brown."

II.
Desiring this order when there are others—
the fox trots through the tiny town,
a branch that has stolen itself and the fire,
and the breasts of the wet nurse fill up suddenly,
she hefts them left and right and offers an opinion:
it is now the baby must be suckled—
and ascends like Crusoe to his cave, that marvelous book
from which one can look out finally
and find the answers.

What's Entailed

It was the only time he mentioned his father. We were pruning
the gooseberries when the thought struck him like a billhook
but he left it to bleed away and die for what had been done
to his sister, the only girl he'd ever loved to death,
half-sister or astral cousin, whatever she was when he whispered
in her ear, keep walking, OK, and
don't look back. Following his own directions,
we weren't allowed to see what course she'd undertaken.

The fox in the foxtail reappears at the bottom
of the town pit, a blaze of orange-red with a white tip
marking the trail back to the previous
love of the future, and would have you too,
an amazed and eye-shaded peer at the horizon,
a new power not to turn myself away
or others at the border.

The Platonic dæmon came thus through a window
I shot a hole in, in the form of a man, a shadow, perhaps in a mask,
striving to be perceived in the yard where we struggled—
that it rained all night erased any question of footprints—
and he promised to return and may yet have done so,
to end my agitation on behalf of others,
and those needed here to maintain the tidewall.
I am too nervous to speak of it now, and beg you to understand
I remain convinced of whatever happened.

4

My Summer

What is it we're mourning now? The adjunct light
had a firm grip on the hospital, or the rooms in it.
The light rose into darkness
just as we wished it, and the love of the child
came of it, but as the flight of birds, a robin
from the pool that formed in the corner of the field
after consistent storms, the dirt pressing up against my feet,
and wasn't that a not inaccurate description
of the sudden appearance of leaves that budded
and pushed out over the course of months
consuming time, the primary sequence,
leaving us to marvel and admire and love
the perennials and succulents and the annuals
worst and most of all, planted from our own dumb hands,
and remind us of the nails born needing to be peeled back
or chewed off in the mother's mouth, if she listened to what we told her.
But the neighbor leaves his big black truck running,
the train whistle booms across the plain,
and then it appears, a way to go on that doesn't include our ideas about it,
the chirr of birds increasing, the dog barking
as yesterday at the end of its lead, what the Greeks called a chain
and celebrated where it touched, cold as summer,
the underground river restored to the sharp-edged
canal on which the sun sparkled, bordered by people
not becoming either, thinking about oxen and asses.

I Know You Are But What Am I

He went outside and a tree fell in his mouth.
He became a root. A boy grew out of it.
I died at that point, like I was buying a house
or my most private thoughts made a sound,
and were public. But for all the burning in the face and genitals,
there was nothing in that day I could touch,
and that was the day I realized it.

The daisies lay single-eyed on the grass clippings.
It wasn't the same as being lazy.
I can be here in four minutes.
It's the point at which a three-dimensional thing comes
to seem three-dimensional.
I am the succulent, the little tombstone reads,
I grow in the brightest indirect or curtain-filtered light.

The robin stood in the tire track and pulled a worm out.
I thought of the thread on my t-shirt,
and for a minute I too seemed alive
like a child or an impression. Acres of water the dam held back,
the brow of shade and light, the flicker of interest,
a mouth like a tent in a rainstorm,
I loved it here, and he was those things,
just as he said we were.

THE SONG OF THE EAR

In the new and awful light, terrible for what you make me know,
I'm not dressed yet, in a certain way. But you were yesterday,
and that carries over until I see you.

Where did the stranger come from? Like all people,
we had never seen him before. And then he was upon us
like snow over willow leaves when it's thin,
though later the surface became unformed. I'm going to leave,
and then come back. I want this place
exactly as before. Remember the blank look
he gave you, which made you smile, and him return.
So the hot man wishes for the cold, though it can't find him
and the chill has slowly set in,
as if I'd accepted I was going to be a fate, and now I needed
to find the one upon whom I would descend.

And though nothing had been done to me
I too felt I needed rest, or rather, was able to,
not like a man who grows fatigued watching
men working in the fields, but as one who has attended
an ecstatic moment through the afternoon
so far away and bright, like a hawk's cry to one attendant in the park,
and knows the other is closer than who he was
and thought to be. The gilded room inside a book,
whose walls grew intangible as the sun went down
it seemed. Or so I read and after I had stopped
to be was understood.

The hedge, not solid with leaves, and yet impenetrable
shook with the thought of sparrows, sharp-toed,
who sing in a minor chorus, not more and more themselves,
nor more than themselves, but their selves becoming more,
as their singular audition can't drown out the others
in a final unity. Stopped, angled like the slash that breaks
a line in a scholarly book, or joins ideas, that scraggly pine
the wind bent to the hill along the coast,
as looking back one sees the way one took
and follows it, arrives, a head in a lap, for good.

THE SOURCE (IN ADDITION TO SPEECH)

The feeling takes several shapes in my head—
I find in describing my own beauty I saw you
and your beauty, a third creature, with a rotation
like a robin's head, that sought to take us all in.
The night the bailiff couldn't come we slept together
as a way to understand other people. The bones in the arm suggest
a machine a little more when uncovered. But there I was neither
alive nor dead, holding you between my legs
on the great voyage, hating the lewd jokes of the bargeman,
until we returned no more changed than the child
(where else has he been?) in time or the dæmon
who assaulted me the night I tried to explain
free love with reference to a terrifying description
of your face, and mine like it.

The language of being together we'd gradually learned,
and tried to forget. What babies we were. I said my lines,
and when we reached that point again, a tighter fit,
I simply repeated them. In the morning the snow was trampled
where we'd looked at birds, and the mud showed through
in anticipation. When it was falling, the snow on the junco's head
played the part of ardor, then terror the footprints, mud
juvenescence. That summer followed the river to its source
and reached it at a marsh, where a canal left the quest
unfinished. And had we done it tomorrow?

The new moon was in the sky, almost blocked by July corn;
a few clouds brightened the stars with their passage;
this my mind inside another's. Wild numbers of fireflies
made diagrams. I wanted to say I couldn't read them,
but I'd been here before, and the grain rushed as if magnified
by a glass or a sudden movement forward of the head,
a desire to see close the years of labor and lose them
in the recovery of their spirit. The face in all the segments,
eyes and teeth, emerged from its unity. I am seen
to be intermittent, open to a general reading
in which I alone am excluded, having settled on a leaf.
I told this by stopping dead, to which I add this epilogue.

Not Dead, Not Dream, Not Poem, Not Faggot

Dream from the middle of the night I was supposed to write, where are you?
Reggie Clark who wore his knitted hat inside and outside also,
who was always late, taught a strange geometry, came to homeroom from the window,
taught foul shots all follow through and saying, *like a faggot*, no tension, knowing nothing,
as he put it, what survives of misunderstanding understood and remembered as mistaken
in a dream that can't be love, that can't write, because the not dead beloved,
ghost of two weeks, ten years, two lives, or how many
wooden afternoons can't hold a pen to the air to the ones in Hades
exactly, more, because they are returning to themselves already,
as the comic's fake kiss aims his back at the viewer, who laughs later, and later
waking from a dream to the opened oven smell of it, warm from that
and formed, and then its apprehension, to lie awake and think about money
not paid, after thinking the poem not written, to loaf and think
that love isn't love that wants its money, the poem isn't the poem not written,
that the foul shots got better late, alone, not mattering, no man or hat or *faggot*
in that motion, except as a memory, a misunderstanding understood
in the wrong word and all lost time from that time not written
contained wrongly but contained into a motion knowing nothing, like all poems,
and all poems not written, Reggie Clark and all the not dead my beloveds?

WANDER HAMMER

Deep in middleopolis the screws untighten
and drop to the floor of the boys' bathroom.
The secret is revealed, the stepmother in a halter,
the shadow on the rug, they were all connected
by a thin tissue of the lies of the father,
like snakes in the grass, harmless garters,
things still themselves after hours.
In identical houses where the beams were visible
but not exactly structural, you leaned against the mirror
like a leaf against the lake and dimpled surface
while the ducks watched from the duck-blind,
and sang the underwater chorus breathing
fresh clean air and sunshine reed-stripped
of a glamorized inversion. Justice. It was so unfair. The sea walked backward,
a new frontier was lowered into place, the usual sunset,
the little shells went twinkle, twinkle.

THE EXTERNAL EAR

And there it was, like a storm-surge or an ornament
half-inflated by its gizmo, not frighteningly human.

We recognized ourselves in that deception,
the one true like a table tilted sharply

until the bowl in the dark stars below the pears is visible,
pitted and grained and nothing falls off but the scales
are folded and put away, for that single use only.

The thought I suggested you had stays with me—
I attach so much importance to what I'm given—

a man with a hooked knife paused from pruning.

Embrace was a word first used of forts,
until the one body fell down inside the other body, and was lost.

LOSSES AND COMPENSATIONS

I went into the other world. A little at first,
a finger in the occult, for now we called it that,
and then the whole body, the spirit, disarming
the paradox of the phlox and brown-eyed Susans
and wild carrot clenched first or pinned and coiled
intermixed with open palms and Queen Anne's Lace
as if being in two worlds at once was just such
a subdivision of identicals, at different stages, as a field of those
differences seemed beside a bedspread or bolt
of cloth unfurled for purchase. It may need to be cut at first,
so later it may be whole again. By then
the paradox had diminished to the point I looked at a tree
with a dazed expression on its face, nowhere to turn
or spend the placid, leaf-still afternoon,
and the boys slowed down to see you breastfeeding
in the dry ditch, and sped away too.

I wonder if you felt some sense of loss, looking
at the tree that way, as if having slept with a man
or a woman you must resign yourself from the double world,
and so be left with nothing, the two overlaying each other
like sun in "a bucket of clothes-pin" at noon.

Without That Inside You

There are birds and flowers
and green and growing things also. One branch hangs low
as the wind has fractured it. But it's the past you look forward to:
just today a hummingbird flew from the center of the road,
leaving an empty space where a bright green leaf had lain forlornly.
I don't think I can say it more plainly. Then I lost it in the corn
which by this date in May had its final proportions.

HOMŒOMERY

I tried to reconstruct the plots of all the novels I could remember reading,
(the prisoner lives on thin gruel but it's a boat
on which he cannot leave the island)
and the plays of Shakespeare, until her face appeared
in the flesh, or air between winter branches, or distant choirs
late for an appointment.

And I loved them, those two, as had always been intended.

5

The Pursuit

I left them both there, stepping out of the kitchen as a cave,
into the afternoon sun and an ever-greater multitude of shadows,
the half-human ones of the washing, the trees even more so,
cenotaph of the barn, and lace of raspberry canes cut back to winter.
What a lie it all was to speak of as being surrounded by conditions.
People carry pictures into the apartment below and the tree
grows up through the treehouse, holding it aloft, and sheltered.
I had at long last come into my maturity, the book reads,
though I already knew it would never be received; it is not
that sort of novel, or life, this being a biography, lines which
embody the subdued and limited desires of my maturity,
opposite citation, the pustules about to burst,
and daily life with its fictions (change has passed like rust
scraped from the stakes and covered with rust-resistant
paint the color of rust, to be driven in the ground beside the young
trees that have grown so and taken on leaves as to almost
have become sails, thus subject to the wind) and true

unhappiness (the shadows of the leaves are flat on the wall
of the cave that is the surface of the Earth to the visible,
as hair lies down around the face in spring curls
dark and lively with August humidity) can't advance
into the sublime evening canyon of every night,
combining gulfs and heights into the graph of a flat line
on graph paper, itself covered with faint green lines,
like rows of corn seen through a screen (though the wind
makes them bow like a covenant and touch) and accepted
like a summons which says you must be available to appear,
which to have glanced at or taken in hand is to have
agreed to, a common law notion that seems to have been waiting,
even sometimes evading or denying, your arrival at its door
where face to face it can't possibly refuse you.
One is finite, after all, the body
replaced by a quadrangular column of the proper proportions,
a bust atop it, by the wayside, someday to be cast down and mangled,
later to become statues, now responsible to the human form.

The Prince

Delirious in the mouth of,
there was rigor in the shoots and pity in the blossoms.
It's not nice to sit in there and watch the day evaporate,
but what she said was,
I knew the sun in Roma in the thirties.

The child is delirious too. In a mouth false with milk solids,
an autistic statue of himself has been carved with a timetable.
We held a leaf up to him as a mirror
and he crumpled it in a tiny fist tiny
to make it ours.

Things presented in reverse order,
the fire, then the black and green of spring,
was what the dream advised
to make May whole again.

A SPLIT-SECOND WHEN GENDER DIDN'T MATTER

Inside the red tulip,
black and yellow,
two bodies laid the same direction
two trees made fertile,
and the bee of difference clambered.

The head went first into the soil,
the tap root followed,
a pearl in the cool pit, warming,
awaiting, repetition.

On the Manners of the Ancient Greeks

                    Long nights I dwelt upon the tainted.
Chamomile crushed by car tires lent its fragrance.
She wanted to get the stains out of his work pants,
the rust-resistant paint, the natural juices of the product.
I described your exuberance on my knees to those letters' branches
that stretched us out into an act, false fruit swollen,
life-sustaining flower, the pronoun.

THE AUTHOR AS READER

The soul in the dream stands for a boat turned over,
the dinghy, Dunkirk, the green light filtering from the depths
the dream reads as normal, the camera as green. Neither is
as it was explains the recording angel
on the table, over breakfast like the boat
was over the light that penetrated anyway.

I was wrong about this also. In the dream's
green light I went down to the river
and couldn't recognize.
The boat turned upside down didn't sink.
It trapped the light and the air trapped it.
Your face pressed into the water for a long while,

a child's while, while the soul keeps floating.
They agree the past can't be separated. The night continues
in the green light of the tipped boat. The occupants,
ferried upside down and backwards, are a past life
a duck in the grass scatters a whole flock of,
different paintings in the house by the river.

The new whites and greens suggest relations
are the same, between different people.
You remind me terribly of someone I knew once,
with the same name and figure,
while you did whatever you were doing.

DOING THINGS

A woman is an abstraction
but Lady
Chatterley runs around naked in the rain and goes
down on the gamekeeper and
equally he her eagerly.
Finally they separate, only to become farmers and lovers.
Going down is what Zarathustra did, leaving
his animals on the mountain.
I sleep with a dog, it's true, but
just the same I've left
Karl Marx Allee to avoid the
longitudinal like the parted Red Sea of concrete flats
made that way to give everyone a place
no one can take in without disappearing in and out, living instead
on the outskirts in Berlin's city center.
Perhaps the sunken ship blue of the ceiling
quiets this awful fear.
Robots greet you with an un-
steady human gaze.
Tomorrow I'll go see the deleted scenes
unless the river sweeps the house away in the
voluble first spring of
winter's summer
x-factor,
Zeno and his crate of halves.

At Home and Abroad

Spring is an old thing where the hill diverges.
He knew he was missing something in the morning
that would always be there, why it hurt. Having eaten

the fruit started to describe him,
then grew into a blur, a vague good sound
like the sea seen through waves of air
to have more waves where you might have looked,
faint-headed, down the path.
The grapes along it are smaller
than the holes in the fence, larger than
the hand and mouth.

The door of beads clicked their colors. The flies
didn't enter, the sounds and the shades.
He wasn't afraid of her.

Ardor, a Declension

"This summer is so much sadder than the other."
–Vladimir Nabokov

Sliding backwards on ice (having seen that I would stop
at the beginning of the next chapter and having continued
through the first few sentences, revealing X, in the form of
a stout lad in a blue jacket, bowing to my beloved)
in an academic police car, formerly corner of Y and Z,
miraculously turning the car 180 in order
that back became front, and I could navigate
more easily the reversal, woven (not forgetting
the dream's agency) through the familiar, oncoming traffic
with headlights whose icicle arrays burst into diamonds
the sky was chock full of. And two scorpions, who walk backwards
and sting forwards, I crushed with a chair till they broke
into smaller, more deadly pieces. The jade
leans over and new growth straight up out of the hurricane-
horizontal palm of its mistaken direction ascends.
Dear sister, I've rescinded my promise
inside the other world,
inside of this one.

SONG OF INNOCENCE

Is there a garden in the sky? The cows stare at the walker.
The horses chase slow-motion. I stood in the sandy slush and watched them.
Snow sends down roots. Good girl to kick him.

A building rises from the brow of every hill and animal,
you included. We live in this invisible building, you can see it,
a room to correspond to every part of the body.

The smaller contains the larger. Red snow falls on the cardinal.
It's water frozen in the shape of your mouth. You're speaking.
The innocent pick it up from the sidewalk,

wear it, eat it, pass it from tongue to tongue
lovingly crushed and bitten. The dove brings back
the flood in its mouth, the abject terror

of white garments on a black floor, and we welcome it, a skull
that touched us, the chairs in the station covered with bird-lime.
It follows us to the hinterlands. Your voice listens

after the evergreens. At the motel a channel
to Patsy Cline has opened. Did you order this,
the cute young guy in the corner, who's been waiting and waiting?

There's nothing to be sorry for. A greeting or a welcome.
The indoor pool is filled with the irregular shapes of children.
Not violated enough, I ask you to repeat it.

CHEKHOV STORY

I got thinner and thinner until I turned into a wire,
something to keep the cows in the field, though deep down
I never think they want to leave it. She turned into the fire
and watched her life pullulating in the embers,
almost disgusted until she remembered, it's burning.
I don't live here, only renting,

throwing the money out the window like heat
through a hole rent in my garment by a willful ember.
But that's me. Deep down I'm on fire, remember.
The cows at the end begin to panic. How is it my eyes
open now only in terror? Why her,
but the waltz is heard by no one on the wireless.

Like my life it hasn't been invented.
She buried her face in her voluminous skirts, and slipped out the window.
At last she was alone. The wind whistled through her,
kicking a few more embers squeaking into the snow. To be doused forever,
something is beginning. The cows groaned in the barn.
They'd been moved inside for winter.

TENTH BOOK

The tradition is sad without you here.
In the past they were alive
like a snake with a head and a tail
at opposite ends of its body and the sky
scrunched up until affinity. Now the moss chases the forest
very slowly through the forest. I picked up a book

to call you, and read about a fly-blown chandelier,
a bit of lilac, the crooked legs of chairs,
while the child of the moment and eternal spun
the landscape where we sat and watched,
together again, the sparks of laundry
from which the body had finally been shorn.

The king was free in a cart to be dragged
through the streets below the rooftops.
A note in the form of a kiss passed
through the barricades. I wasn't alive before,
I thought it said. It's the steps that talk,
bright snake, while nothing starts.

6

Own Memory

This is not for deceptive purposes. I don't know what day
or year I'm living at the Read Cafe, no one more dear
than the other, even if it fell out of a novel, like a bookmark
in New York constantly turning to marriage.

She wasn't possible. The character in the novel
like a character in the novel refused the offer,
offering the red-winged blackbirds singing
for sex in the cattails, when it doesn't belong to asking.

If opening actually made the red appear,
like a ticket or a token on a windshield,
then the green of fiberglass is made of grass, and somebody else
has taken the picture, somebody where we've ended up together,

the point of light being an unfinished kiss, where you stood in the room
of the big pink chair, before it started to exist.

Epithalamium

There was a crumpled iron barrel.
I recognized him from somewhere.
The sun behind a stand of timber, an iron brush
colored with horse hair. I saw you looking at my bracket.
Your look was made of whalebone.

Once, the sky spoke to me. I wrote down words,
feeling it already slipping out of my grasp
into my lap. There was a woman with two bodies.
The weeds pointed at the ground in winter.
I wed one thing to another

until I was alone, on a plateau with the water tower.
Having lost track of the alphabet at L, M, N,
O, they couldn't find it in themselves to kill him.
Death will be like an open grave inside
of life which is infinite and fills everything.

The Seed of Projection

Penis and tulip candled on the ceiling,
not the shadow category called you or I wanted,
like an impure thought provokes an action
it doesn't recognize: what it really wanted freed
as the red-winged blackbird showed
the hawk into space, below the new black field,
far from its nest,
the woman who doesn't want to be tied up
by the hands that lifted almonds and raisins
to a mouth that had forgotten
the grosbeak balanced on his mate until there wasn't
any difference.

The Silence of the Press

The boy's bookish knees pried open the roots,
the flowers wilted in the shape of his hands—
a rose of stone may have dropped its petals.
Day might now await the night without regret.
He'd been taught to await their appearance,
dismayed and eager, where the tomb had been.

A boy finds a puddle with his stick
and it's erased. Good. Another turns,
but her friend has passed her. The rough stone wall
released into a grove where the bee-eater dipped,
and wandered away through the transept.

A Suitable Credenza

The war came after a couple of mistakes,
but the star found us visible in the tragedy
by which we would return to our former selves with new lives
having banked on the reverse.

We lay in the grass long enough,
heads toward the dark,
for it to break a little before getting up.
Skin in the morning sun cast light

instead of shadow as a man
gave birth to a legitimation problem
solved when someone recognized you as a stranger
among the men and women.

The regularity of this passage frightened.
Ducks clustered around the only hole for miles
in the river's ice, like a Greek tragedy's audience,
the actors lost beneath the current you noticed
the slight wind had again defeated.

THE MIRACLE OF SUN AND SHADOW

The yellow jacket took the injured
yellow jacket back to
the tree to eat it. You tell me
to leave the door open so
you can hear the singing.
The boy was moved by
the mortality of three
sisters when one died and
a drawing of some purple loosestrife.
The smoldering leaf piles
burn the present. The yellow jackets
on composted apples,
the feeling of great events
pulling back into the station
now a meadow with a retaining
vault of sky below it
where a star rose in his notebook
the door had closed accidentally
though religion and the odyssey held it open
with small *o*s and consonants
so the cat could enter and leave
without disturbing the night that had come
eventually to be the one promised
long after you knew it to be so.

LISA'S STORY

The horse lets you see
the hole in its side where it's snowing
and the cart goes free.

ALTERATIONS

It's the map of the house
you spent years reconstructing,
but the leg that breaks, the stranger that can't

stop talking, the snow that doesn't fill the woods,
the ground unwhitened, your sister and brother
unclothed by the horses. The white makes them frisky,

the fear of death walk into the woods
with that stranger inside you, a word the trees miss
in their entirety. It keeps them from the paddock,

with the cloud in the lake, among the questions
around your legs and fingers.
The children raise their arms and wave in Xs.

Golden Fruits, Golden Isle

I.
In the sealight I feel sick
and like to think, if it were happening now,
as is,
how would it be organized, that it could.

Like many sweet things it had appeared rotten.

Like a configuration
of waves and clouds in the hands of a skilled maker
turning the wood he'd been saving for years into a vibration,

forced to retreat to the portable shelter, happy to be alone
in the period between the birth and the death,
the most memorable in the history of the world.

II.
The ruins of the new days of summer
obscurely suggest the whole fragment,
the grandeur and perfection of the life,
and the wind called to move it.
A tractor on a collection of concrete blocks and scraps of wood
seems more poised than ever.
Thinning peaches answers this need in the child to wait
to do the thing it isn't capable of,
and in that sense will never be
the dark and extravagant fiction of a beach
that masqueraded as an island, a woman
in dubious relation to her husband—she sent him
inland, a few feet—offering the dull and twitching feet
to the sea, square and perfect, which answered the individual
with the system and the sequence that allowed it
into all her variations.

The name, lacking an object, completes it.
Famously, the blue cloud dissolved into the sky while you were speaking.
The umbrellas became skeletal after the storm repelled us.

A day of perfect balance

that had to be caused by something,
the sun, that old pun, in a moment moved
neither closer away nor further,
again its own antecedent,
the genuine secret by which you meant
small grapes from a young vine,
dark and viscous, taken through the diamond
of a chain link fence into the mouth's triangle
beside a steep path to the Mediterranean,
the one sea one went further into the world to get to.

Inappropriate Method

The water goes back into the water,
bend down to see the moon through the window.
I shouldn't have eaten, I shouldn't have
felt the breezes. I'm not a duplicate
of the man you didn't marry. The spy smiles
at the mailbox, he smiles at noon.
I couldn't refuse to feel the current,
the current couldn't hear your confession, you didn't
give it, just said it, said the wall is
a piece of the universe, I'll face it.
Thank you, I'm a sundial. I've forgotten
how to fold the crane daily
that lifts me while I hold it
to understand the failure of leverage
in the abstract, shiny, polka-dotted foil.
Directions for directions turn me over.
Spring's a button not to be pushed but buttoned,
to which each part naturally attaches,
the crane in the palm of the tree,
the leg falling out of the sun-scarred table
to the floor like a rattle, and the body,
one's own singular body.

Persuasion

I don't recognize myself these days.
How did I get so beautiful? The dead have a presence
and consciousness, but no personality, no other world
to interfere with this one, or get lost in.

Why is sleep erotic? And how else return?
And on this cold dry night the skin
on knuckles cracks, and more stars are visible
than in summer which had been reported

to be full of life, and was, so little does it change
because we do. There are papers on the floor
that must contain a word that can be in the ear
without approval, yes or substantially or I have an idea

that will do for the next two minutes, easily.
Afternoons are regrettable, otherwise, but stunned
by the presence of the one left hours ago is the night
the dead pass, and what's left to try to talk us into.

OMNE SCIBILE

The biography confirmed I didn't write down
what happened between us.
The wallpaper in Peter's bedroom
showed the revolutionary war,
and I went home while he was sleeping, still unsure.

There were many things I came to prefer. The mental world

with its bright scar where they took out the difference
between right and wrong,
as if without preference.

A memory of being cruel calls up another
wind-like force it is possible to feel paradoxically,
as in a small high school or silvery-green hay.
Her knee pinched his genitals a little like a gaze
and held it while she slept until he felt recognized

in the smallest movements, a sharp warmth,
breeze through the hedge with a trace of the branch,
as if most moments weren't already cruel and benign,
the breath on his face. As if that were the end.

There was also a flower I held between my legs
in search of moisture, held firmly by the waist
and swam toward sunlight,
though later it was moonlight off the crests, still later a bedroom,
a chair with a black spot (resembling the terror read aloud
to the finish) where somebody's head had continued.

And then I went back to look for it
where the sea recited and sent me, on my way,
which wasn't its, though it was the same,
as we were born in the same year,
distant, near the beginning of that now ended war.

THE BOOK AT HOME

Thinking it was done I turned around
and the downpour was at my door,
blocking the path to the ferry, and the boy
began to make the movements of what had gone before,
an arm in a salute or patch, a poor
attempt at running into space
a river bend or choice between what was
and what had gone before would make.
I was sitting on the couch.
I was imagining the dead boy gave me strength
or the accident gave me life
or the coincidence of the return predicted choice.
The kitchen turned
to face the door. The angel said,

the days were infinite before I knew how to pass them.
My club foot ached when I forded the noon
or the cobbler's sign was a shoe
of solid wood too big for wearing,
when I knew it speeded up in the narrows,
becoming nearly a cloud, but with unenviable force
everything that can speak
speaks against you,
thinking about what it will become
when it's over, which leaves the tree you can climb out
the window into, a watering can reflected in a puddle,
the color of a very determined
heaven, the seasons in the beech hedge ontological,
copper leaves carried green to winter.
And I promise to lie if anyone asks me about you.

Roadside Bouquet

Is a sin the same in the mind, the first of summer?
Yes because what are we but language, as geometry
is a language of objects in space, and a sin
of objects in space, a language where we could have met,
and did, and carried on like phlox, as the Dane put it,
wondering if an erotic life could possibly coincide
with the forgiveness of sins and the age
one must acquire. But the schoolmarm wasn't satisfied.

Is it time to stop writing the poem to be a poem,
making the shapes that make one (the reader) think of a poem,
cutting words out of pure blue and purple sheets in bed
to be applied to the page in ways that suggest space,
responsible to that, like the sheet of newsprint
rubbed against the stone with crayon or charcoal,
or instead of that? The problem of a dream:

the vacuum was on, despite protestations,
so no one heard me say this but the teacher.
Earlier from the stack of papers with names
it hadn't occurred to me to take my own,
and having this pointed out tried to appear foolish.
A different language: I knew the man in the room

was going to come out into the house and attack
the occupants, try to kill them, and I was frantic
because I had already read a long article about this.
I'd come from the future. It occurred to me as an explanation.
But maybe instead he'd come from the past,
bringing with him the terrible and horrible
feeling of recognition, as if even this had been subject
to a prophecy: this is how I arrived here, looking

around the new apartment, phlox sagging by the window,
curtains dragging the carpet, just as was foreseen,
for has been seen, at the moment the sound of the approaching
train's whistle enters and is so huge as to become interior
and whistle too small a word for this, looking out

from the sound to the light that hovers above and in front of
the train and the track impossible to see in the dark:

it is the recognition one is looking at, the massive engine creeping it down
to be filled with grain or emptied,
and, a god in every word, what difference remains.

A Scythe Laid in the Grass

A horse interrupted our kiss, she said. I was always hearing
those noises in the intense desire to communicate
the flight of something (it was a moth
whose movement of the creatures
is unpredictable) instead we discovered in a stalk of grass
not far from where we sat bathing, largely white,
no bigger than had seemed to us in progress,
which gave pause in finding and noted triumphantly
that it was quoted from the gospel of Luke,
despite its revolutionary appearance as we headed
for the low ground: E. M. Forster's *Arctic Summer,*
in which one was exposed as a twenty-year-old body
below a melting hierophant. I like you, too,
without intention, as I insisted nevertheless,
in which the hard peach was marked
with your initials, leaf, a worm-hole, natural bridge,
pure yellow and orange of a sky after storm clouds.
But the way it looked had never been enough
to get there, to be human (turning the pages
and serving airy dishes) until we seemed so.
Who we are was yet again what followed.
"Darling, it was so hot I rode my horse into the sea,"
you wrote. "The war keeps ending."
Not everyone understood this to be the future.

The First Sound They Hear

Though how they can sleep through it remains
a source of pleasure, making them stop like a ravine
in an ordinary wood upon reaching the meadow
where the features of the land are equalized,
the only question they have then being how to get home
without returning the way they'd come.
Isn't there a circuit back through those trees,
where Wally showed the Large Tree Society plaque
on one of the world's largest oaks, to get them back
by a new route? He was a strange man, and happy
in a way that I have never met him again.
Meanwhile they'd found their way into the bed of the glen,
and the blindfolded one lay in the stream,
the one who'd led him from behind
cradling his head where he'd let him fall.
They are a few of the names known to all,
and fewer still of the minutes, and more of the days
and seasons, the winter to whom the footsteps belong,
growing in size while they remain constant, hence smaller,
like the leaves on the oak or the plaque's words,
though they react as if they were real people,
as in fact they are.

Acknowledgments

Thanks to the editors who first published some of these poems in: *American Letters & Commentary, Boston Review, Colorado Review, Conjunctions, Court Green, CROWD, H_NGM_N, jubilat, Konundrum Literary Engine, LUNGFULL!, Poetry Salzburg Review, Slope, Verse,* and *Volt.*

This book is given, with gratitude, to its readers—especially LF, the first.